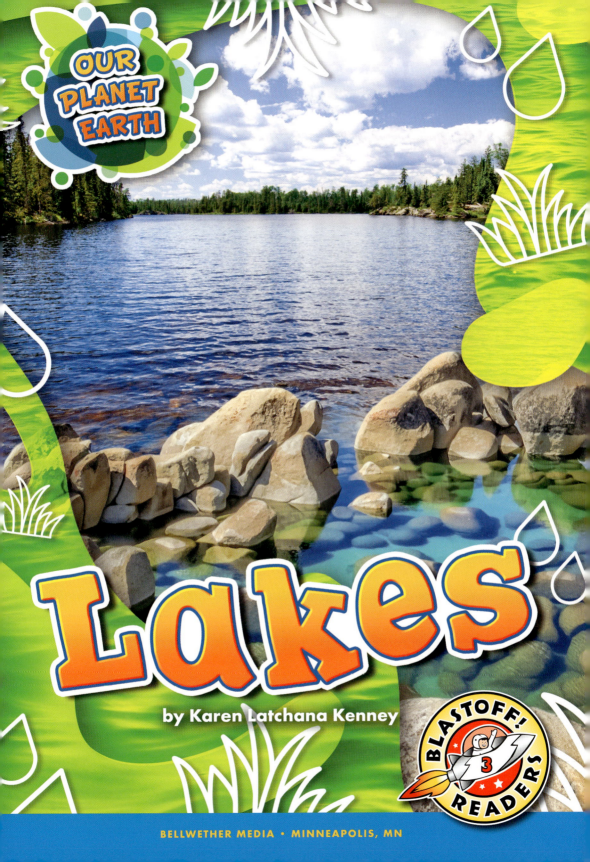

Lakes

by Karen Latchana Kenney

Blastoff! Readers are carefully developed by literacy experts to build reading stamina and move students toward fluency by combining standards-based content with developmentally appropriate text.

 Level 1 provides the most support through repetition of high-frequency words, light text, predictable sentence patterns, and strong visual support.

 Level 2 offers early readers a bit more challenge through varied sentences, increased text load, and text-supportive special features.

 Level 3 advances early-fluent readers toward fluency through increased text load, less reliance on photos, advancing concepts, longer sentences, and more complex special features.

★ **Blastoff! Universe**

Reading Level

This edition first published in 2022 by Bellwether Media, Inc.

No part of this publication may be reproduced in whole or in part without written permission of the publisher. For information regarding permission, write to Bellwether Media, Inc., Attention: Permissions Department, 6012 Blue Circle Drive, Minnetonka, MN 55343.

Library of Congress Cataloging-in-Publication Data

LC record for Lakes available at: https://lccn.loc.gov/2021045041

Text copyright © 2022 by Bellwether Media, Inc. BLASTOFF! READERS and associated logos are trademarks and/or registered trademarks of Bellwether Media, Inc.

Editor: Kieran Downs   Designer: Laura Sowers

Printed in the United States of America, North Mankato, MN.

Table of Contents

What Are Lakes?	4
Plants and Animals	12
People and Lakes	16
Glossary	22
To Learn More	23
Index	24

What Are Lakes?

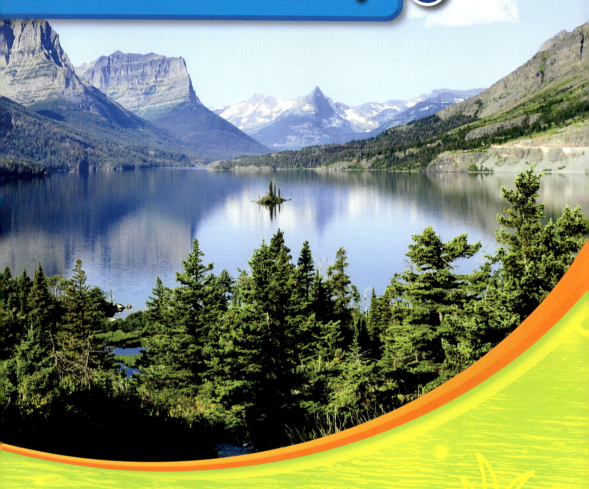

Lakes are bodies of water with land on all sides. They can be many different sizes. Lakes can be very deep or shallow, too.

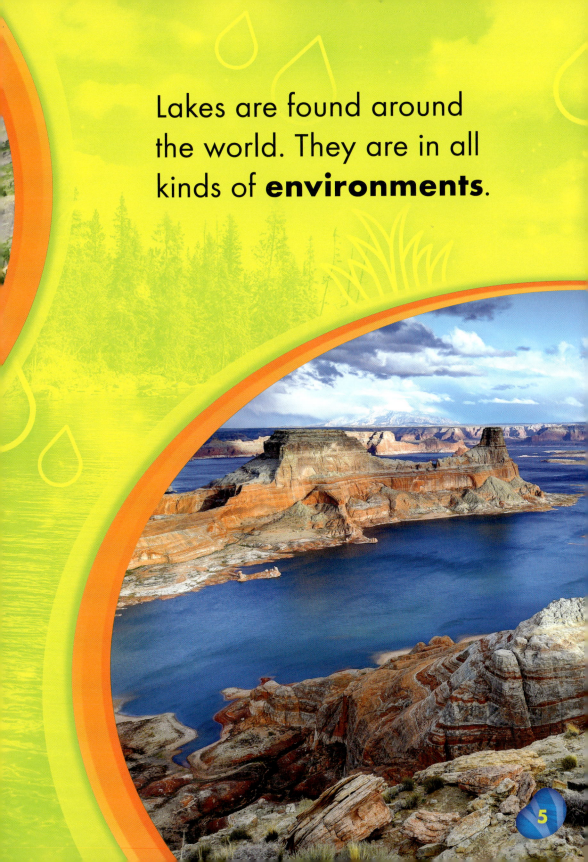

Lakes are found around the world. They are in all kinds of **environments**.

lake inside a crater

Lakes form when water fills **basins** in the ground. These basins form in different ways.

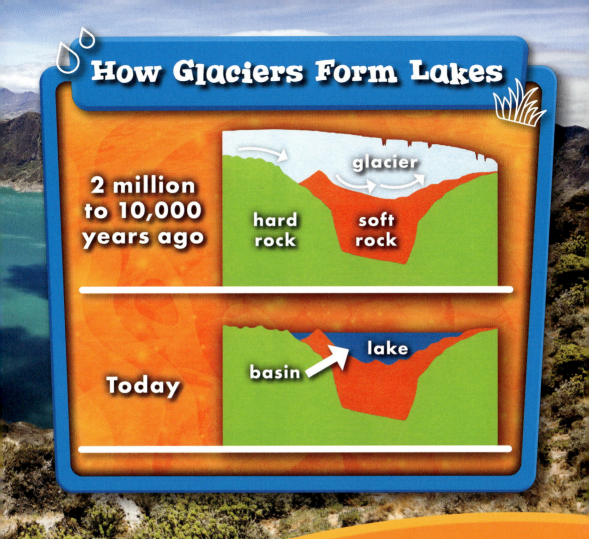

Volcanoes form **craters** that can fill with water. **Glaciers** scrape basins into the ground. Cracks in Earth's **crust** can also become lakes.

Many lakes fill with rainwater that collects in basins. Melting snow and ice can fill basins too.

Lake Baikal

Famous For

- Deepest and oldest lake in the world
- Has more than 1,500 animal species

Size

- Covers 12,248 square miles (31,722 square kilometers)
- More than 5,300 feet (1615 meters) deep

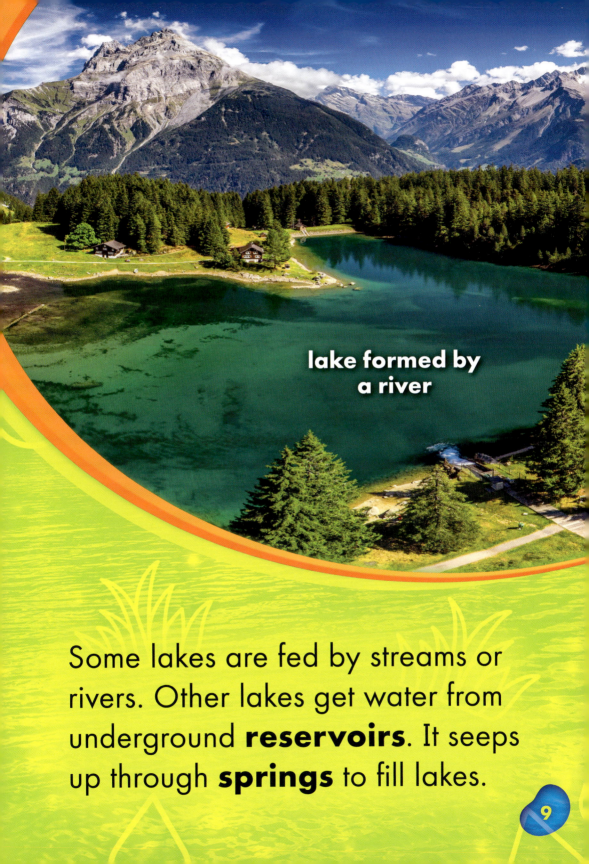

lake formed by a river

Some lakes are fed by streams or rivers. Other lakes get water from underground **reservoirs**. It seeps up through **springs** to fill lakes.

saltwater lake

Lake water moves slowly or stays still. Most lakes are freshwater. But some can be saltwater.

Water flows in and out of open lakes. Closed lakes only have water flowing in. The water leaves through **evaporation**.

Great Salt Lake

Famous For

- Largest salt lake in the western half of the world
- One of the saltiest inland bodies of water in the world

Great Salt Lake, Utah, United States

Size

- Around 1,700 square miles (4,403 square kilometers)

Plants and Animals

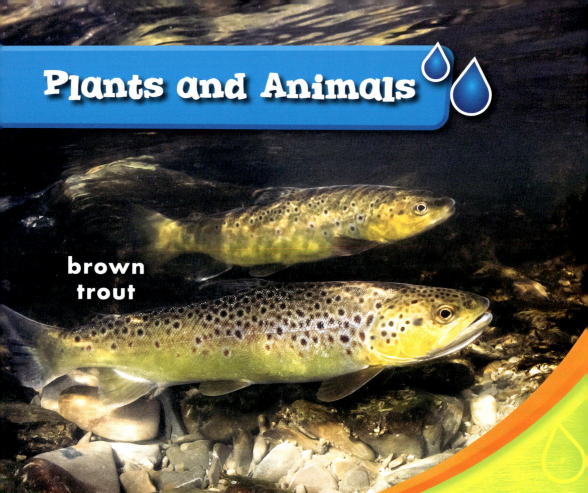

brown trout

Many plants and animals live in or near lakes. Trout and catfish swim through duckweed and water lilies. Mayflies and dragonflies fly above the water.

Ducks paddle through floating **algae** in the water. Snapping turtles munch on worms and water moccasins.

wood duck

Deer and elk drink from lakes.
Beavers find sticks to build dams.
Eagles pull meals from the water.

Lake Animals

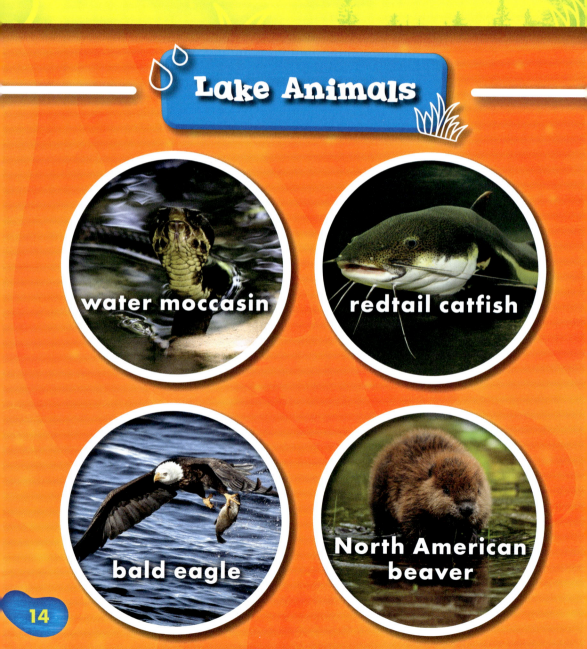

water moccasin

redtail catfish

bald eagle

North American beaver

least sandpipers

Frogs snap up moths, spiders, and slugs. Sandpipers eat beetles and worms by the shore.

People and Lakes

People use lake water for farming and drinking. People also use lakes to ship goods and run power plants.

Lakes are used for fun as well. People enjoy swimming and fishing.

fishing

shipping goods

invasive species

pollution

People harm lakes. **Pollution** gets into the water and makes it unhealthy. Boats carry **invasive species**.

Climate change causes changes in weather around lakes. This can raise or lower water levels.

How People Affect Lakes

- Pollution makes water unhealthy

- People bring invasive species into lakes

- Climate change makes water levels change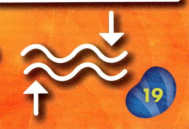

Many animals need lakes to live. Lake water keeps plants growing. People need and use lakes every day.

People can help lakes by keeping them clean. It will save our lakes for the future!

Glossary

algae—plants and plantlike living things; most kinds of algae grow in water.

basins—shallow, bowl-shaped areas in the ground

climate change—a human-caused change in Earth's weather due to warming temperatures

craters—the hollow bowls at the top of volcanoes

crust—the outermost layer of Earth

environments—the land, water, air, plants, and animals that make up areas

evaporation—the process when water heats up and turns into a gas that goes into the air

glaciers—large masses of ice that slowly move across the ground

invasive species—species that are not originally from a region that cause harm to their new environments

pollution—substances that make the earth dirty or unsafe; pollution usually comes from humans actions.

reservoirs—supplies of water underground

springs—areas where water flows from underground areas to above the ground

volcanoes—holes in the earth; when a volcano erupts, hot ash, gas, or melted rock called lava shoots out.

To Learn More

AT THE LIBRARY

Green, Sara. *Rivers*. Minneapolis, Minn.: Bellwether Media, 2022.

Murray, Lily. *Hidden Habitats: Water*. Somerville, Mass.: Candlewick Press, 2021.

Rivera, Andrea. *Lakes & Rivers*. Minneapolis, Minn.: Abdo Zoom, 2018.

ON THE WEB

FACTSURFER

Factsurfer.com gives you a safe, fun way to find more information.

1. Go to www.factsurfer.com.

2. Enter "lakes" into the search box and click 🔍.

3. Select your book cover to see a list of related content.

Index

activities, 16
animals, 12, 13, 14, 15, 20
basins, 6, 7, 8
climate change, 19
closed lakes, 11
crater, 6, 7
crust, 7
drink, 14, 16
effects, 18, 19
environments, 5
evaporation, 11
farming, 16
formation, 6, 7
freshwater, 10
glaciers, 7
Great Salt Lake, 11
ice, 8
invasive species, 18
Lake Baikal, 8
land, 4
open lakes, 11

people, 16, 18, 19, 20, 21
plants, 12, 13, 20
pollution, 18
power plants, 16
reservoirs, 9
rivers, 9
saltwater, 10
ship, 16, 17
sizes, 4
snow, 8
springs, 9
streams, 9
volcanoes, 7
water, 4, 6, 7, 8, 9, 10, 11, 12, 13, 16, 18, 19, 20

The images in this book are reproduced through the courtesy of: Wildnerdpix, cover; FloridaStock, p. 3; Don Fink, pp. 4-5; worldswildlifewonders, p. 5; Noradoa, pp. 6-7; Katvic, p. 8; Eva Bocek, pp. 8-9; vvvita, pp. 10-11; Marco Regalia, p. 11; Rostislav Stefanek, pp. 12-13; Robert Vandenbeg, p. 13; Rafael R Sandoval, p. 14 (water moccasin); Kletr, p. 14 (redtail catfish); Igor Kovalenko, p. 14 (bald eagle); Holly Kuchera, p. 14 (North American beaver); Lonn Garris, p. 15; Dan Thornberg, p. 16; John Brueske, pp. 16-17; Jeff Caughey, pp. 18-19; AnnaTamila, p. 18; jack f schultz, pp. 20-21; Mr. SUTTIPON YAKHAM, p. 23.